I0159343

# The Unknown Quest

## Book 1

An Unofficial Minecraft Series

## By Mr. Crafty

Copyright © 2020 by Kids Activity Publishing. All rights reserved.

No part of this publication may be reproduced or transmitted in any form whatsoever, electronic, or mechanical, including photocopying, recording, or by any informational storage or retrieval system without express written, dated and signed permission from the author.

Disclaimer: This book is a work of fan fiction; it is not an official Minecraft book. It is not endorsed, authorized, licensed, sponsored, or supported by Mojang AB, Microsoft Corp. or any other entity owning or controlling rights to the Minecraft name, trademarks or copyrights.
Minecraft ®/TM & © 2009-2020 Mojang / Notch / Microsoft

# Contents

# Chapter 1

The process was slow. Agonizing. Steve moved forward an inch at a time, wincing every time a leaf crunched under his foot or the grass rustled just a little too loudly. There were a dozen different noises coming from every direction - the soft baaa of a sheep, the disgruntled oink of a pig, and somewhere, a bee bumping into trees and hopping from flower to flower. Hopefully, it would stay at the other end of the grove, where the wildflowers intermingled with the trees, and not make the current situation even more difficult.

It wasn't that it was difficult, really. It was just *agonizingly* slow. Steve was willing to bet all the apples in the upstairs chest that he had seen sheep chew faster than this was going.

This being Steve trying his absolute best to catch the very evasive attention of a small, funny-looking cat. He had barely even seen it at first. Its patchy, multi-colored fur helped it blend right in with the forest around them. Steve *probably* wouldn't have seen it at all if the cat hadn't bounced its way up the steps into town to get a drink from one of the village farms.

"Psst... psst... Come on buddy. Come on!"

There was some tiny part of Steve that knew this was ridiculous. He was a hero. A celebrated one, at that. There were statues of him all over! Maybe he had been the one to make some of those statues, but that wasn't the point! He was Steve, known all across the land for his bravery and skill, particularly with a sword. No zombie, skeleton, spider or *Ender Dragon* was going to stand in his way.

"Mrow."

Yet, somehow a cat was getting the best of him.

"I have fought things a thousand times your size," Steve grumbled, slowly creeping forward in a crouch. Before long, he wasn't able to get any closer without jumping up the hillside. Exasperated, he straightened up - just in time to watch the cat hiss and dart off into the weeds.

Again.

Steve threw both arms up with a loud sigh, and then immediately set to scolding himself.

"Well now you've definitely scared it off! Good job, Steve! Some hero!" He glared out into the growing dark. "Can't even make friends with a cat."

The dark. Frowning, Steve took his diamond sword from his back and peered around into the shadows created by the many, many oak trees. There didn't seem to be anything to worry about just yet, but there would be soon enough.

Once dark settled over the valley, it wasn't long before monsters began to slink around. Steve always thought it was rather stupid of them - hadn't they heard of him? Perhaps a skeleton gave him trouble now and then if they caught him by surprise, but bah!
Nothing hidden in the forest was a match for Steve, particularly if he had on his diamond armor.

Which he didn't.

"Shoot!"

Steve began to move a little faster, sprinting up the hillside and towards the distant torchlight of the village. He was much further away than he should have been. That was the kind of mistake he couldn't afford to make too many times, but Steve hadn't realized how far he had gone until he was running back. The cat had kept him perfectly distracted, lured him far from the safety of his mountain fortress and the village below he sought to protect.

"Stinking cat! It won't happen again." Steve vowed, speaking loudly to nothing. Well, not entirely nothing. Just as Steve reached the wooden fence that encircled the village, he heard a low, grumbling groan off to his left. "Oh, no you don't! No one surprises Steve!"
That wasn't entirely true either. He couldn't help but jump, letting out a small shout of alarm as a zombie appeared behind him. Of course, where there was one zombie there was almost always another one!

What were you thinking, Steve??

Fortunately, Steve's sword was more than a match for them, cutting through the zombies with a single hit. A lump of rotten flesh bounced onto the ground; an item Steve opted to leave behind. It wasn't good for much, and it *smelled* terrible, even more so than Villager Brian when he forgot to take a bath. The second zombie popped into smoke with a loud moan as Steve hit it squarely in the head. He grinned smugly over his minor success. "You've still got it, Steve!"

And, of course he did. He was Steve, after all! Hero of the land! Builder of enormous castles and fantastic statues, protector of villagers, slayer of zombies, defender of –

"Hey!"

Speaking of statues. Steve had fashioned a likeness of himself in the middle of the village, constructed carefully from wool, dyed to match his own clothing and skin color. It had taken ages, and he had walked for days looking for flowers to make the right dyes, and *now*

The enderman didn't seem to notice Steve's shout, occupied with plucking out a block of blue wool from the bottom of the statue. At least, it wasn't going to go like the first time, Steve thought. That brilliant work of art had been made from sand.

With an enderman around, it hadn't lasted very long. It had taken ages to fix it up, and Steve wasn't looking forward to the idea of having to repeat the scenario and go flower picking *again*. Picking flowers just didn't seem like a very heroic thing to do.

Although he had to admit, he did like how the tulips looked in the flower pots he had made from clay a few weeks ago.

"Hey! You! Get lost!" Steve sprang forward, waving his sword dramatically from side to side as he avoided looking directly at the enderman. He didn't want to make him angry, after all, just scare him away! Still, the creatures had a nasty reputation for grumpiness.

After a few seconds of fruitless threats and shouting, Steve came to the conclusion that the enderman must be hard of hearing. He would have to get creative.

Scowling and grumbling to himself, Steve hopped up onto the front platform of his fortress, where several chests had been placed wherever Steve could find room.

One of these days he would do some spring cleaning.

Tomorrow, maybe!

"It's not even spring." Steve mumbled, fetching his desired item out of a chest, and walking back down the cobblestone pathway to the statue and the culprit. A criminal, as far as Steve was concerned! These creatures, beings who showed nothing but disrespect, had forced his hand. It was time to take drastic measures.

Steve stopped at the well, dunking his bucket inside. It infuriated him. This entire thing was going to make such a mess, but unless a thunderstorm conveniently came through, what other option did he have? Steve stood just uphill of the enderman, clutching the full bucket between his hands.

"Sorry, Mr. Enderman sir, but this is *my* village and *my* statue, which means-" Steve paused for dramatic effect before tipping the bucket over in front of him. Water began to fill every square, rapidly seeping forward and running downhill towards the statue.

And the enderman.

"You need to leave."

The reaction was almost immediate. Water flooded the space, knocking over weeds and spilling seeds out across the dirt. The enderman turned his head sharply, eyes widening, his entire body jerking back and forth in a rapid, alarming motion. If Steve had never seen it before, it might have scared him.

Right now, it was just satisfying.

In the blink of an eye, the enderman used his teleportation powers, vanishing from the place with a loud screech. In the distance, a villager who had been walking outside took the hint and scuttled into his house, slamming the door sharply behind him.

Smugly, Steve moved closer with his bucket in hand, using it to scoop up the rest of the water and leave the cobblestones as they were before. They didn't seem to be damaged, and if anything, were a little cleaner now! He deserved something for that, didn't he? An extra apple from the rations pile, perhaps. Steve beamed, looking over his handiwork and silently congratulating himself on solving the problem without actually fighting the enderman. As everyone knew, endermen are fast and dangerous, and that just wasn't a risk he needed to take right now.

Something became heavier in Steve's chest the longer he surveyed the scene. The houses, the road, the statue.

The statue!

The enderman had taken the wool block with him!

# Chapter 2

"Argh!!"

Steve was livid. Didn't that enderman know how *hard* it

was to get blue dye out here?

It wasn't that difficult, honestly. Perhaps he was just looking for something to complain about, because he was bored, but STILL! He would have to go out into the woods and find more flowers, and he knew better than anyone that cornflowers just didn't grow around here. There were poppies everywhere, but he had *never* seen a cornflower. Who knew how far he would have to walk to find some? Present Steve was more than a little irritated with past Steve, who had decided it would be silly to make a flower patch out here. To be fair, the sheep probably would have eaten them or something, or the ENDERMAN would have walked off with them.

Better a flower than his statue blocks though, Steve thought, scowling out into the dark. He swore, just for a moment, that he saw a pair of white eyes out there in the night.

The flowers would have to wait until morning. He was *not* getting turned into a porcupine full of arrows just for some stupid flowers. Wasn't there some other way to make blue dye? At least, Steve thought, it wasn't a green block. There weren't any cacti for days, and if Steve really thought about it, he wasn't even sure where the nearest desert *was.*

That was a problem for another day. Cacti were much easier to grow. Maybe he should take a trip and get a few and set up a little cactus farm. It would also double as a security barrier against more endermen, maybe.

Could endermen pick up cacti?

Wait! Lapis lazuli! Steve's expression brightened. Perhaps he didn't have any cornflowers, but he DID have lapis lazuli, and by the chest full. It seemed like every time Steve turned a corner down in the caves, the blue speckled block was there. Eventually he'd stopped even bothering to mine it, just because there was so MUCH of it, and really, how many uses did it have?

Humming a little tune to himself, Steve began to bounce up the stairs towards his home. The magnificent, mountain fortress was his best work, no doubt about that, and he was including *all* his statues in that statement. Carved into an enormous mountain, the front entrance was carefully constructed from sandstone and colorful glass panes. Mostly blue. He had to do *something* with all that lapis lazuli, after all. Maybe, Steve thought, he would spend the next week gathering other dye ingredients and making a glass tunnel to the lake at the eastern edge of the forest! That would sure be something! The sun would look amazing through all that glass, and perhaps the villagers would enjoy it.

Not that Steve would ever really be sure. Standing at the mouth of the fortress, he could see a good dozen of the folks walking around the small village below, "hrm"-ing and "hrn"-ing at each other.

He had tried to communicate. He really had! Once Steve had settled into retirement, he decided he needed a break from working on the fortress. Steve had grabbed a couple of pork chops and a few bundles of wheat to trade and headed down the front staircase to the nearest villager; a baker, from what he understood. Browsing his wares, Steve saw mostly bread and eggs, both things that Steve could make just fine on his own.

Of course, he was a busy guy and he didn't *normally* have time for that kind of thing, but now that he was retiring, settling down, so to speak, he thought he should at least get to know the neighbors.

The villagers seemed to largely only care about emeralds, trading for them and giving them away in exchange for other supplies. Steve himself had no use for emeralds, and he couldn't think of anyone who did. Besides, he didn't have many emeralds. He had so much leather and exactly zero need for things like leather armor anymore (he had a full set of diamond armor in the fortress, for Steve's sake!) so why couldn't he trade them a piece of leather for a cooked chicken, or something like that?

Overall, it didn't seem to make very much sense. Steve had spent a long time trying to explain that to one of the green-coated villagers who didn't trade *anything at all* and had gotten nowhere. Not even the villager with the purple coat, clearly the brains around here, seemed to understand when Steve came to him. He just hrmed and hrned and made little sense to Steve, so he had given up.

Every morning, Steve left the fortress to head out and gather supplies in the forest, and as he walked through the village, he was always sure to wave and say hello.

The villagers always gave a firm 'hrm' in response, which Steve had decided probably meant hello back. It could have meant literally anything, of course, since it seemed to be the only thing they said. Sometimes the sound was a little louder, softer, or accompanied by some movement.

None of it meant anything to Steve. Trading was the only thing the villagers were good for - he didn't even get experience for hitting one.

Steve grimaced. He'd tried it once and didn't feel good about it, but he had been desperate. He had been starving, and the villager had food for trade, but without emeralds …

When the villager vanished in a puff of smoke, there was no food! It had been a waste of energy, and it riddled him with guilt every time he thought about it. Steve had spent the next week and a half gathering wool from sheep in order to make a Steve statue as an apology to the village. He had even used a real diamond block as the core of it and had made the base out of glowstone blocks so that they could easily find it in the dark.

Steve considered this village home now, and had surrounded it with a small wall, topped with fencing to prevent spiders from climbing up and over. It didn't stop endermen from teleporting in, apparently.

Cacti. That had been the original thought. Steve could put a little cactus fence around the village and maybe that would … definitely hurt the villagers. Steve had noticed pretty quickly, genius that he was, that they weren't very smart. Particularly the fellows in the green coats, who didn't seem to do much of anything but walk around and get in the way. Once, Steve had been trying to get a bucket of water out of the well and one of the nitwits (it was a clever name, Steve thought) had knocked him into the water! Steve had been lucky to have his pickaxe on hand but breaking out of the well had flooded the lower part of the village and destroyed some of the farm plots.

Steve could see them from where he was standing now and couldn't help but grimace a bit. He never had repaired those farm plots, had he? Oops. Maybe he would work on that tomorrow…

Lapis lazuli.

"You're getting sidetracked, Steve," he mumbled to himself, trying not to dwell on what it meant that he was talking to himself. "Time to repair the statue!"
There was still time before he went to bed.

Humming once again to himself as he walked, hopping up and down through the halls and watching the torchlight bounce around, Steve thought about the fortress. He had spent weeks on it, and even now he grew bored and had started making new rooms. He had a furnace room, and two or three storage rooms, and then above that there was the 'top part' where Steve had spent hours upon hours fighting with redstone blocks to try and make an automatic furnace.

Redstone mechanics still eluded him. All it took was one misplaced block and he risked blowing up the whole room. Once, Steve had miscounted the number of blocks from the furnace room to the storage room and almost put down a line of redstone into his TNT room.

It probably wasn't very smart to have an entire room of live TNT, but it looked cool, and to Steve, that was all that mattered. Besides, they were nowhere near his bedroom, so even if he'd been blown up he would have been fine!

Actually, the more he thought about it, the more entertaining it sounded. Maybe instead of looking for flowers that's what he would do tomorrow. That *definitely* sounded like more fun than getting his hands stuck full of cactus needles.

Eventually, Steve found the stone storage room, carefully decorated with color-coded chests and displays of the different ingredients found within. It had taken a lot of wood, but every chest had a sign on it as well. With so many different kinds of supplies to be found within the mountain, Steve had thought it best to label everything in some way or another.

His eyes jumped from one sign to the next. Perhaps he should have sorted things differently. Alphabetically, maybe. Oh well, too late now.

Steve eventually located the stack of chests labelled LAPIS LAZULI and popped it open.

He blinked. He closed the chest, reread the label, and opened it again.

The chest was empty.

# Chapter 3

How could it be *empty?* Baffled, Steve closed the chest and began to open the others in the stack. Empty, empty, empty. All of them were empty!

Steve furrowed his brow and slowly moved down to the next set of chests. It wouldn't be terribly unlike him to have come back from a mining trip and been too tired to check the label on the box, right? He was a busy guy, with a lot going on. He had probably just been so sleepy one night that he had put all the lapis lazuli in the wrong chests.

That had to be it.

One by one, Steve went through every single chest in the storage room. After that, he went to the next storage room, just across the hall, the one that had all his glass. Perhaps he had gotten ahead of himself one night and already made a bunch of blue glass!

Those chests were empty too, and so were the chests that should have held any blue wool he had made.

"Roger!"

Steve closed the last chest, the echoes of creaking hinges chasing him out into the hall. At a full-on sprint, Steve made his way down the labyrinth of hallways, his memory serving him well. In no time he made it out of the fortress and back to the village where a single villager was still out on the plaza despite the late hour.

Of course, there were no zombies to worry about, what with the wall. So, what was there for the villagers to fear?

Right now, the answer was Steve. The human stormed down the front steps from the main entrance, charging towards the villager with a scowl across his face. It had to be Roger the nitwit! Who else could it have been?

The green-coated villager looked up from his favorite activity of ringing the alarm bell over and over again, after hearing Steve's furious shout that every mob from the village to the far jungles could hear.

"Roger!! You stole my lapis lazuli!"

Roger the nitwit stared blankly, hand raised to give the bell another firm smack with his closed fist. He blinked. "Hrm?"

"I know it was you, Roger!" Steve bumped harshly into the villager, knocking him back. "I told you to stay out of my fortress, and I told you to stay away from my stuff!"

Roger frowned. "Hrm."

Winded from sprinting all the way from the storage rooms to the village plaza, Steve took a few seconds to inhale a porkchop and exhaled furiously. Roger stared back at him, blinking a few times. The villager inched forward and raised his hand again. For a split second, Steve could scarcely believe what he was seeing. Roger the nitwit was going to hit him! He had a fist up! Out of reflex, Steve grabbed his sword, holding it out in front of him in warning.

His hand continued to rise.

Roger smacked the town bell once more, the sound echoing all across the village. The one other villager who had poked her head out promptly raced back into the safety of her home.

Ring, ring, ring, ring –

"Stop it!"

Steve slapped Roger's hand away from the bell with his own, placing the sword back on his back and scowling. Heart still beating furiously, he began to circle around Roger, examining the pockets of his coat closely and finding … nothing. A single piece of lint fell out onto the ground.

It was a stretch to think that Roger the nitwit had stolen from Steve's storage rooms, but who else could it have been? The nitwit was the only one Steve had ever seen inside the fortress - although Steve had reprimanded him fiercely on that occasion. None of the other villagers were stupid enough to dare go snooping around through Steve's things, not even to look at the mushroom farm he had growing on one of the lower levels.

But who else could have done it? After all, Steve was the only human in the world of Minecraft. There was no one else.

No one.

Not for the first time, Steve sighed heavily. He turned away from the villager, mumbling an apology to Roger who merely hrmed in response. Steve took the stairs back up to the fortress.

The walk back was slower this time. He didn't understand. Could he have put the lapis lazuli somewhere else? Could an enderman have teleported inside and taken the entire chest? It had never happened before, but it was the only thing Steve could even fathom. After all, he was the only human in the village, the entire *world*, so who else could have taken it? Steve frowned, thinking about the little calico cat that had snatched a piece of fish from his hand and bolted.

Yet he knew as well as anyone that a cat had no use for lapis lazuli, and he had never seen one anywhere close to the fortress. While the cats didn't seem to mind the villagers, they were wary of Steve. Perhaps they thought he might hurt them?

"It had to be that stupid enderman," Steve grumbled, scowling. Next time, he wouldn't just dump a bucket of water on him. No, next time he would take out his sword and really show him who the boss of this world was! Steve, the hero!

Steve, the only builder in the entire world.

# Chapter 4

Not for the first time, Steve woke to the sound of a bell ringing. He knew it well - particularly after Roger had spent so much time banging on it right in front of him. Was the villager trying to drive Steve up the wall? It wouldn't be hard. Lately everything seemed to get on his nerves.

*You need a vacation,* Steve thought. But to where? Where would the world's only builder and hero go on vacation? Perhaps he could travel through the forests and visit the distant mushroom isles, or to the jungles far to the south. The idea wasn't all that appealing. He had already seen mooshrooms, and they weren't exactly the tastiest of creatures. He had already explored the ancient temples that were hidden behind curtains of vines among the jungle trees. Perhaps he could go off the coast and see one of the warm water reefs and build a fantastic new home out of coral.

He would have to get all the water out of the way so that he could put blocks down to build. Just thinking about it was making him agitated and he wasn't even out there yet.

The bell clanged again, and with a groan, Steve rolled out of bed, pausing only at his chest to get out his sword and a shield. There was no reason to wear full armor, unless there were pillagers, which never happened.

It happened. Steve walked out the front entrance of the fortress, stepping from shadows into sunlight, and paused. Just past the gate, he could see the banners held high.

*OK, Roger. That was a good reason to ring the bell.* With another loud sigh, Steve turned around and returned to storage, getting out a set of armor as well as a few bundles of arrows.

"Where's my bow?"

Steve looked around, exasperated, and began to check the other chests. In a purple chest labelled "Spare Wood," he found it. No, not his bow. It was definitely a bow, but not his. His had a brilliant shining color to it. *His* glowed with powerful magic. He was more than capable of taking out a pillager with a single arrow if he hit him just right.

This was just a plain old wooden bow, without a speck of magic in sight.

Frowning, Steve took the weapon from the chest. No time to be *picky*. The pillagers could cause trouble for him if he allowed them to hang around, but he couldn't risk killing them near the village either. Somehow - magic, maybe? - the other pillagers always got wind of what had happened, and word spread all through their own villages and watch towers. Before too long, a full squad of pillagers would show up and burn the village to the ground.

With an arrow notched into not-his-bow already, Steve began to walk back out to the front entrance. The pillagers had opened the gate and were now standing near the plaza. Roger the nitwit was running in mad circles around the bell, now and then pausing to smack it firmly a few times. Perhaps he wasn't a total nitwit after all, Steve thought, watching him for a few moments. Perhaps Steve had Roger all wrong. Maybe the villager was actually very clever.

Maybe he was just bored and that was why Steve kept catching him doing stupid things. Steve could understand that. When one had saved the world, most other activities seemed dull by comparison.

But Roger hadn't saved the world. And right now, Roger was running straight for one of the pillagers, hrming away as he went.

All thoughts that he and Roger could become friends vanished from Steve's mind. He released an arrow, chuckling to himself as it thudded into the wood near Roger's head and sent the villager scuttling back towards his house with a "hrm!" of alarm.

The pillagers watched Steve march forward with interest.

Steve remembered the first time he had seen pillagers. He had been so excited to see something new and strange, even if they did just look like uglier villagers. He had hoped, against his better judgement, to be able to communicate with them.

Unfortunately, the pillagers seemed to speak a language similar to the villagers, and they weren't nearly as friendly.

Steve had almost been reduced to a puff of smoke by their powerful crossbows.

This was not his first fight with the pillagers, but at least it had made his day more interesting. It was *definitely* better than digging more holes in the ground or going to look for flowers.

Of course, it did mean that he was going to have to head off for a few days until the pillagers calmed down and stopped looking for him. Even better, perhaps he could track the pillagers back to their tower or find it on his own. That sounded like an adventure! That sounded like fun.

Except, Steve thought, what if different pillagers showed up and destroyed the village while he was gone? They weren't terribly clever, but they were smarter than most hostile mobs Steve had come across in his travels, and clearly, they could easily open the gate and get inside. He could always block it, maybe.

The memory of the enderman came immediately to mind. What if more came to wreak havoc on the village? It was so incredibly unlikely, but boredom was leaving Steve's thoughts racing with potential problems. He had spent weeks, perhaps months, working on his fortress and the wall around his village, attempting to keep casualties to a minimum and protect the villagers who remained.

Steve recalled the day the zombies had gotten to the cartographer. Not one to waste anything at all, Steve had broken the house down and turned it into a shrine to the poor man, with a little pond surrounded by sugarcane. Someday, he would replace that with bamboo.

Thinking over his plan, Steve made his way towards the pillagers, scowling deeply at them. It was going to be difficult. He would have to sprint past them, avoid their attacks and provoke them into chasing him out of the village and into the forest.

Steve noticed a sudden movement in his peripheral vision. Not a pillager, not a cat, not an enderman. Steve turned his head, pulling his sword off his back, ready for trouble and finding, well, trouble.

What he saw shocked him so much, everything seemed to happen in slow motion.

"ROGER! NOOOOOOOOOO!"

There was a distinct ping of a crossbow bolt being released. Steve threw himself forward, shield arm out, feeling as if he couldn't go fast enough to protect the nitwit from danger.

"Hrm?"

# Chapter 5

I can't look.

Steve closed his eyes, airborne, arm stretched out before him. It would be a shame if he managed to block the crossbow bolt and instead hit poor Roger with his sword, but his thoughts were moving too fast to think clearly.

"Ugh!"

Steve felt his hearts decrease as the bolt caught him in the chest. There was a loud "HRM?" and the creak of the gate, and then Steve was rushing forward again, pushing Roger the nitwit on with his shield.

"Run, Roger! Run!"

Whether the villager understood him or not, Steve had no idea. He scarcely had a moment to close the gate behind the both of them before they charged forward, Roger hrming anxiously as he raced ahead. Steve was surprised. He'd had no idea that a villager could move that fast. If he hadn't been so angry with the green-jacketed nitwit, Steve might have been impressed.

Right now, there was nothing to do but run.

Roger took the lead, sprinting head-first into the nearby birch trees. Perhaps he was a bit stupid, but right now, the urgency of the situation seemed to stick with him. They were in real danger! Roger didn't even have armor! Or a sword!

"Keep going!"

Steve turned, rushing to put away his sword and shield and take out his bow, notching an arrow to aim at the nearest pillager. They were still much too close to home, but there was nothing he could do right now.

The arrow hit the first pillager, who let out a grunt of pain and jumped backwards. They had such big eyebrows. It was probably a stupid thing to notice, but it was better than thinking about those massive crossbows and the excellent aim pillagers tended to have. This wasn't how he had planned to approach this situation at all.

Normally, Steve would have been careful. Yes, he would have sprinted through them and gotten them to chase him, but he wouldn't have run into the forest! The trees blocked his way, and it was so hard to aim between them to hit anything.

It would be just his luck if the pillagers somehow managed to hit Roger in all the chaos.

So far, Roger's instincts seemed to have kicked in and Steve lost sight of him entirely. Was that a bad thing? It was probably a bad thing. Steve notched another arrow and let it fly, smacking a different pillager in the shoulder.

*Wow, those guys look angry*, Steve thought, racing backwards. "Oof!"

This was what he'd been talking about! The trees were in the way. It was going to get him into trouble!

With difficulty, Steve began to knock away blocks of leaves and even punch at the trees, breaking a straight line through the forest while ducking down and under limbs to dodge the crossbow bolts. At least the pillagers didn't seem smart enough to do the same, and overall were having much more difficulty navigating the forest than Steve was.

"HRM."

Steve knew that sound. That was the sound of a villager, a plain old villager, likely one in a green coat, who was in trouble. Roger was in trouble because... of course he was! Why wouldn't he be? Spitting out a mouthful of leaves, Steve crouched to get under a birch tree, and spotted the source of the problem just ahead of him.

Unfortunately, he realized what had happened to Roger just a moment
too late.

Roger had fallen.

Roger had run out of the forest and had been unlucky enough to find where the world split open, creating a chasm leading deep into the ground. The sound Steve had heard was Roger running forward and slipping over the edge, letting out a grunt of pain as he thudded onto a small ledge just a few feet down.

A ledge that Steve missed entirely. In his madhouse sprint to escape the pillagers, Steve hit the edge of the chasm in a jump.

Oh boy.

This was going to hurt.

As Steve hurtled over the edge, he caught a glimpse of Roger standing against the chasm wall, the pillagers closing in on his position.

Poor Roger.

# Chapter 6

Steve hit the ground with a loud *"OOF"* that doubtlessly echoed all up and down the chasm he had fallen into. Unfortunately, he wasn't around to hear it. The world went dark for a brief, alarming moment. Then, Steve woke up in his bed.

"Well, you haven't done that for a while," Steve grumbled to himself, getting up from the bed and looking himself over. His hearts were full once again, but all of his belongings were gone.

It had been a while. Steve had been very careful not to make any stupid mistakes, even if he knew he'd just wake up back in his own bed, because the walk back to get all of his things could be annoying. That was part of it. He didn't quite understand why it happened, but every time Steve fell from a high place or took one too many arrows to the back - er, front, Steve never ran from a fight! - all of his things shot out of his body like he'd been the victim of the world's biggest creeper explosion.

There was also a limited amount of time to get his things back. Steve didn't know if his belongings merely floated away, were absorbed into the earth, or if someone was taking them, but he knew he had about a minute or two to race back out.

Getting to the bottom of the chasm would be difficult, but not as dangerous as it had been to fall down the first time. As Steve fell, regretting that he would probably never see Roger again, he had caught sight of a waterfall. All he had to do was creep carefully to the edge of the chasm and jump, making sure to land in the puddle of water.

Otherwise he would end up back in his bed, again, and his items - his DIAMOND ARMOR, FOR ONE - would be gone forever.

It wasn't like he didn't have more diamonds in his chest. He could make more, but it was the principle of the thing! Perhaps Steve had settled into retirement many moons ago, but that didn't mean he had forgotten the struggles of being an adventurer, out in the world, dealing with whatever it had to throw at him.

As he walked from his bedroom, past the storage rooms, and out onto the fortress steps, Steve mulled over the first time he had ever found a diamond.

He had been deep down in the caves, living on mushroom stew and the last of his pork chops, fearful that every stray arrow from a skeleton would mean losing what little he had managed to gather. The blue speckled stones shone brilliantly under torchlight, and he had been so excited!

Too excited to realize his mistake until it was too late, Steve had ripped the diamond out of the rock with his pickaxe, and the shining stone had bounced right into the lava with a sizzle.

Steve had vowed never to make that mistake again and spent the rest of his mining trip moving agonizingly slowly, careful to place pieces of cobblestone nearby to barricade his treasures from falling into the lava.

*Poor Roger*, Steve thought again. The pillagers had been chasing Steve towards the chasm, and if he were lucky, one or two of them might have fallen over their edge in their haste to hunt him down. More likely, they had found Roger huddling against the wall, hoping to be forgotten, and shot him down.

Poor Roger.

Steve shook his head, full of sorrow, and bounded down the steps of the fortress and out into the village.

"Hi Roger," Steve said, making his way.

A green-robed villager hrmed and wandered past, making a beeline for the bell, which honestly wasn't a terrible idea right now. The pillagers would most likely come back at some point, so there was no sense in telling Roger to leave the bell alone, after all, and -
"Roger?"

Steve came to a stop, blinking several times in surprise.

"Hrm?"

Roger the nitwit stopped at the bell, blinking back at Steve, one enthusiastic hand raised high in the air and ready to slap.

Steve took a step forward, squinting. It couldn't be. He was probably wrong. Steve always had a lot of trouble telling the villagers apart, but Roger the nitwit was always wearing that stupid green jacket that made him look like a wandering bush.

Perhaps one of the other villagers, hearing news of Roger's unfortunate demise at the hands of pillagers, had taken his coat and put it on?

Ring, ring, ring, ring...

No, that was definitely Roger.

"Roger? How did you get out of the chasm?"

Steve had thought about that too. If he had gotten back to the crack in the world and found Roger the nitwit somehow alive, he would have to dig a staircase out or place new blocks, something like that, so that the villager could get out. Villagers weren't any good at doing that on their own. They just didn't seem to understand building. It wasn't even that hard! Steve had tried again and again to explain it to them, hoping that maybe someday the villagers could build Steve statues all on their own, but so far, no luck.

But right now, builders and nitwits were all the same to him.

He was just glad Roger was here, and alive!

# Chapter 7

"Err… Good job, Roger," Steve said awkwardly, reaching out to pat the villager on his square shoulder.

"Hrm."

Ring, ring, ring, ring…

Hope died. Steve had been thinking, just for a moment, that perhaps Roger the nitwit had been hiding a secret all this time, but now that the jig was up and he had proved himself clever enough to get out of a chasm, he would have more to say than hrms and hrns.

"Hrn." Roger looked Steve over, and returned his attention to the bell with renewed vigor. Was he perhaps trying to warn Steve? The ringing was almost like a metronome, each PING the exact same amount of time apart. Almost, Steve thought, like Roger was counting down to something.

Oh no, his items!

"Bye, Roger!"

Steve broke into a sprint. How much time had passed? How much time did he have left? How long had he stood there, staring at Roger and his stupid green jacket? Steve bolted forward, taking note of the open gate on his way out and the calico cat disappearing into the dark. Wouldn't that be funny? What if it was the cat all along? What if the cat was the one making a mess of everything?

Was it mad at him because he'd tried to give it cooked fish instead of raw?

Steve's mind was a mess of jumbled, half-panicked thoughts as he ran into the trees. So far, so good. No pillagers, no cat, no edge of the chasm. Where was the edge of the chasm?

It would have been incredibly funny if Steve had fallen over the edge all over again. He knew there was no way he would make it back a second time, so instead, when Steve found the place in the trees where he had broken through the leaves to escape the pillagers, he slowed.

The edge of the chasm was there, and to Steve's surprise, there was a torch. Had he put that there? Had he been holding a torch in his hand instead of his diamond sword when he had fallen, and accidentally placed a torch while trying to catch his balance?

That seemed far-fetched, but it was the only explanation Steve could think of in the moment.

Of course, Steve had definitely not made a staircase in his panic as he fell off the edge of the world, but there was definitely a staircase now. Bewildered, Steve moved forward, hopping down the oak stairs and onto the ledge. This, Steve realized, was roughly where Roger had been standing.

There was no time. Steve shoved a hundred questions to the back of his mind and inched forward, looking for the waterfall and finding a hundred new questions as he did so. Leading from one edge of the cliff and all the way down to the bottom of the chasm were yet more stairs.

Steve's mouth fell open in amazement. Could he have been wrong? Could it be that he wasn't the only builder in the world? Quickly, Steve raced down the stairs, just barely avoiding a fall off the side and into the chasm's depths. As he ran his heart sank.

"You're too late," Steve told himself, stopping about halfway down the staircase. Although he was still a fair distance away, he should have been able to see his things laying around on the stone ground, shouldn't he?

Even if some of his things had been thrown into the water and floated away, he couldn't have dropped all of them like that, right? Right!? Steve was saddened to think of all the wasted materials and supplies. His stomach growled. He had sprinted all the way from the village, but he had been counting on those leftover pork chops to keep his strength up to travel back and deal with the pillagers.

The pillagers! Perhaps they had taken his things, and built the stairs? They did have those towers that they lived in, and after all, someone had to have built them. Right? Steve nodded. It was very clear to him now that the pillagers had been able to build all along, and they had built the staircase and stolen his things and ... freed Roger?

"Roger!" Steve shouted, voice echoing off the chasm. He knew the villager couldn't hear him, but darn him! Steve had put all the puzzle pieces together now. Roger had been bait, leading him out into the forest and over the edge of the chasm, so that the pillagers could steal his things! Roger and the pillagers had been working together the whole time!

At this moment Steve turned furiously around, ready to stomp back into town and accuse Roger of one thing or another, when he spotted a chest.

A chest tucked under the staircase, that was most definitely not one of Steve's chests. He would've remembered making it.

Then again, plenty of strange things had been happening lately. First his Lapis Lazuli had gone missing, and then these stairs, and, okay, so like maybe three weird things had happened recently.

Scowling deeply, Steve walked towards the chest, checking carefully for signs of a redstone trap or something. Maybe there was a pressure plate in front of it, and when he stepped on it, a hundred blocks of TNT would go off and blow a hole the size of his fortress in the ground!

Steve had considered doing that once, but it seemed rather risky.

Fortunately, no traps or pressure plates or anything went off as Steve moved forward and opened the chest.

"My stuff!" Steve cried, his confusion only growing greater with each passing moment. Why would the pillagers take his things and put them in a chest for him to find later? That just seemed absurd!

# Chapter 8

"It wasn't the pillagers," Steve said, once again speaking to himself. He did that a lot lately. It wasn't like there was anyone else to talk to. The villagers couldn't answer him in a way he could understand, and neither could the cat or the sheep or anything else.

Hrm.

With a villager-like sound of confusion, Steve began to gather his things from the chest. He noticed he was missing some torches and food, but there were still plenty of both to allow him to get safely back home before it got dark. One important thing was missing, however, and Steve wished that this stranger had taken anything else. His diamond sword was missing, and in its place, someone had left Steve an iron sword.

It was better than nothing, he supposed, frowning.

Brow furrowed, Steve closed the chest and turned to look around. The chasm stretched far in either direction, leading into the side of a mountain to the west and stretching almost at an angle to the surface going east. The westward path seemed to go further underground, and the cave was dark. Whoever had done this had not gone that way, that was for sure!

Or, Steve thought, they were much braver than he was, going into a cave without leaving a path of torches.

Steve shoved the thought aside. No one was enough of a moron to go into the caves without torches. Of course, they could always use a night vision potion to get around down there, but those were so difficult to make. Plus, there were already monsters down there, and without light, more would spawn!

If someone were that much of an idiot, Steve wouldn't waste another moment of his time wondering about them. After collecting his things from the chest, Steve spent a few moments putting his armor back on. It was a little damaged, but not nearly as bad as he had been worried. There was one question still nagging him though. He hadn't seen the pillagers on his way out, but he hadn't seen any crossbows or anything on the ground either. Whoever had built the staircase and freed Roger might have killed them, but what if they hadn't?

Or, Steve recalled, it had been the pillagers all along and they weren't actually as bad as he thought. It would make sense, maybe. Steve had never seen them attack a village until he had attacked them first, although they would definitely fire the first shot given the chance.

Steve winced at the memory of a crossbow bolt hitting him in the back. Not very heroic. Who shot people in the back like that?

He did, sometimes, but that wasn't the point! How else was he supposed to win a fight with a Ghast? Shoot it while it was looking at him? No sir, not Steve! If he wanted to continue to be a builder here in the world, he had to stay alive! To stay alive, one couldn't expect to fight fairly with a Ghast.

Or a blaze, or the Ender Dragon or ... Okay, so a lot of things required less than fair play, but what else was he supposed to do? No one told stories about the hero who traveled through the end portal, showed up in the End, and ... died. No one cared about Steve the builder.

Steve arrived back at the village, watching the sun set behind the fortress as he wandered through town. Roger was nowhere to be seen, leaving Steve wondering if he had seen the villager at all. Or maybe he had seen a ghost!

Steve grimaced. He had never seen a ghost. There were skeletons, and zombies, and once, long ago when Steve had been wandering through a mushroom forest, he swore he had seen Herobrine.

He hadn't. It had been an enderman, Steve told himself. That's what those eyes glowing in the dark had been. It was strange though, that the enderman hadn't attacked him when he looked at it, but Herobrine surely would have attacked as well!

"Herobrine isn't real," Steve mumbled, scowling at one of the villagers as he wandered past. Everything seemed in place, he noticed. Nothing weird, nothing moved around, no animals where they shouldn't be.

Steve exhaled, not even realizing he'd been holding his breath this whole time. Everything was fine! He was getting all worked up over nothing. Perhaps, Steve thought, it was time to take a break. Even though it was dark, he had plenty of time to work on something to settle his nerves. This was his retirement! He was a hero! He had his own statue, for Steve's sake! He had slain a dragon and defeated countless enemies and built a mighty fortress that rivaled the great buildings found in the Nether.

He deserved a break. That was what all of this was about. He had been a hero, undertaken amazing adventures, and now it was time for a break.

Was he already so bored that his mind was INVENTING reasons for him to be worried?

A sheep inched past him, working its way towards the field of wheat.

A sheep.

"Argh!"

With a cry of annoyance, Steve raced forward to grab a bundle of wheat and use it to lure the sheep into following him. "How did you get out?"

"Baaa."

"Baaaaaa to you too," Steve replied, walking backwards up the stairs and into the fortress. More than once the sheep lost interest, and Steve had to follow it carefully to herd it back into the fortress. How had the sheep gotten out? Abruptly, Steve remembered he hadn't seen Roger for a while.

Oh no.

"Baaaa." "Baaaaaaaa." "BAAAA."

He was going to need more wheat.

# Chapter 9

Steve eventually managed to corral all the sheep in their underground pen. It was a nice place! He had worked hard on it, digging out an enormous area underground and then digging all the way up to make sky lights so that the sheep could have some real sun once in a while. The builder had spent ages making a fence they couldn't jump over, placing hay bales in strategic locations, and even making a nice little pool of water for them. He had even gotten lily pads! Did the sheep know and appreciate how far he had to go to find lily pads? Did they know about his fierce battle with a witch? Did they know his sadness when he failed to tame her little black cat?

Of course not. They were sheep.

"Baaaa."

The sheep didn't really seem to care about the lily pads at all. Sometimes they walked on them, and fell into the water, and sometimes they got a little bit stuck. Maybe, Steve thought watching one bob around in the water like a fat white fish, he ought to remove them. It would be a shame if something happened to the sheep, and it wasn't like they needed the lily pads.

That brought on an idea. Steve spent a few minutes clearing out all the extra things from the pond and cutting down a couple of the trees he had planted down there. Aboveground, the trees provided shade from the sun, and a comfy place for the sheep to take shelter from the rain.

Down here, Steve thought, it was just kind of idiotic. The sun didn't even light the whole room up through the glass windows, and the rain couldn't get in at all.

So, they didn't really need the trees. Steve gathered up the saplings that fell as well as an apple from one of the little oak trees, crunching on it happily as he made his way down into the fortress. He had an idea! If he wasn't going to be out adventuring anymore, then he needed somewhere nice to sit and relax, all by himself. Somewhere, Steve decided that the villagers couldn't get to him.

It was during that train of thought that Steve realized he hadn't seen Roger inside the fortress either. The gate to the sheep pen had been open, allowing them to roam free and eventually wander outside, but there was no sign of whomever had opened the gate. It definitely hadn't been Steve, he knew that. He would have noticed the sheep before if he had accidentally left it open, and it had been several days since Steve had last visited the sheep pen for wool.

Someone had left the gate open. It hadn't been Steve. It hadn't been Roger.

Could an enderman open a gate? Steve frowned. He had never seen one do it before, but then, how much time did he spend watching endermen?

So many strange things were happening lately! If Steve didn't know better, he would think that someone was playing a trick on him, but no one in the village was prone to that sort of thing, were they?

Steve followed the fortress tunnels until he reached a dead end he had discovered some time before when he had been working on making a few new mining shafts. Deep inside the mountain Steve had broken through a stone wall and found a lake underground. There weren't really many interesting ores in the cavern, and the lake itself was large enough to swim in but not big enough to warrant making a boat.

It would make the perfect fishing paradise for Steve to make use of in his retirement! After a long day of collecting supplies and mining coal to stock the furnaces and repairing the fences around the village, Steve could get his fishing pole and come down here and relax. It was a brilliant idea! Except, Steve thought, there weren't any fish to be seen in the lake.

Hm.

"I'll just have to go catch some fish," Steve said out loud, his voice echoing around the cave. That would make a fine project! He would expand the cave, smooth out the floors, and set up a little fishing dock out on the water. Once everything was perfect, he would go catch some fish to put in it!

Steve bobbed his head in agreement with himself. He was so smart. So clever!

After all, he was the only builder in the world, so it reasoned he would be the smartest person in the world as well.

"Yep," said Steve, watching the water for a few moments.

Eventually, he set out to work. Steve took a few torches out of his bag and began putting them on the walls, carefully counting blocks so they would be exactly the same distance apart from each other. It wouldn't do to have his new cave paradise look messy, no sir!

Proudly, Steve stuck the very last torch to the wall.

Directly next to another one.

"Aw, shucks." Steve scowled. He must have miscounted. Of course, he had!

Why couldn't anything go right? Wasn't it enough that he had saved the world or something??

Okay, so maybe the dragon had been trapped in the End, but what if it had escaped somehow? Then the world would have REALLY been in trouble. Also there had been that Ghast, one time, that had SOMEHOW squeezed through a Nether portal and appeared in the overworld. Steve had taken care of that too! Like heroes are supposed to, Steve had taken out his bow and arrow and shot it down.

Sure, it was his fault the Ghast came through the portal in the first place. It was his portal, but that was beside the point! It could have come through any old portal. There were old ruined portals all over the place!

Except that Steve was, as everyone knew, the one and only builder here in the world, so it had to have been him, right?

There were the Nether fortresses, the end portal, the mineshafts down far below. Once upon a time, long, long ago, there had to have been others. "You're not the only builder," Steve said to himself, brow furrowed. That was the only explanation.

Perhaps, Steve thought, the world could only have one builder at a time. That would make sense! With as quickly as he could build, it would be silly to have more than one. The world didn't need more than one. After all, there were still structures left lying around from the last builder!

Steve began to work on the cavern, now and then making trips to the furnace to melt cobblestone down into its natural state. The cavern would look more natural, he had decided, with real stone floors and walls instead of elaborate pillars. Anyone who came upon it would simply think it was a relatively normal cave.

Except, you know, all the torches and everything. It wouldn't really be much of a very peaceful cave if there were a bunch of zombies everywhere, and the floor wasn't going to stay very flat if a creeper blew a hole in it.

At least it wouldn't be a supercharged creeper. That would really mess things up for him! Steve had seen it happen once. He had been out in a massive field when a storm rolled in, thunder rumbling so loudly he couldn't even hear the whinny of the horse he had been trying to tame. Before Steve could make a run for it into the nearby forest, lightning began to strike. It hit the trees, the ground, and then far out in the middle of the field, a creeper!

Unable to resist the urge to investigate, he crept over to the creeper with the strange blue glow. Steve had woken up shortly after in his bed. He wouldn't be doing that ever again. It had taken him all day to walk back to that field, and by the time he got there, all his belongings were long gone. That was assuming the impact of the creeper's super charged explosion hadn't blown them up in the first place, or that lightning hadn't burned it all up. The one lonely tree that Steve had seen in the fields had burned down entirely.

Steve spent some time caught up in his own thoughts, thinking over the adventures he had had so long ago. Some weren't even that long ago, to be fair, but it sure did seem like it as the days went by.

It took all day and another night to finish fixing up the cave the way he wanted it. He made a pathway of lily pads over to a small island, and even planted a bit of sugarcane on the far side of the cave in some sand. Did the underground caves usually have sand? No, but who cared? Steve was probably the only person who would ever see the cave, so maybe it didn't matter if it was a natural cave or not. He changed his mind a hundred times as he worked, even going so far as to replace the torches with redstone lamps later on. They looked out of place underground, but they were pretty, and again, WHO CARED! It was his retirement cave, for Steve's sake! It could look however he liked!

As Steve made another slow walk out of the cave and down the hall to the furnace, he heard an odd sound. A flapping sound, a loud, almost leathery, weird noise. It was a sound that Steve had never heard before. Which was saying something, because Steve had heard a great many things in his many, many adventures.

After some walking around, Steve determined that the noise was coming from outside! It was Roger. It had to be Roger. Steve pursed his lips and began heading towards the front entrance, trying to decide if it would be better to lock Roger up somewhere so he would stay out of trouble, or if he should push him outside of the village and lock the gate.

Probably the latter if Roger really was working with the pillagers.

Hoping that it *wasn't* a pillager attack, Steve headed outside.

# Chapter 10

It was not pillagers, and it was not Roger. The moment Steve stepped out into the night air, there was a terrifying shriek from above. Steve realized that the flapping sound was caused by wings. Wings! Something was flying above his head, and now it was diving down to attack him!

"AAAHH!" Steve shouted, reaching for his sword. Although it wasn't enchanted like his old sword, Steve was glad he had taken the time to make a new diamond sword, even if it meant using the last of his diamonds. The mobs up in the air were strange, nasty creatures, with teeth and glowing eyes. For a moment Steve thought they were tiny dragons, out for revenge after Steve had killed the big one, but no! They were something else entirely.

The first died, dropping something like a membrane when Steve hit it a couple of times with his sword. On a second look, Steve realized the creatures were leaving behind some kind of smoke as they flew, and to his horror, more were spawning. Again and again, Steve struck them down, getting a better look at them in the light of the torches around the village. They were blue, with eerie green eyes, and their backs seemed to have some kind of bone-like pattern to them. No, Steve thought. Not a pattern at all. The actual bones of the creatures showed through their patchy blue skin! These were undead mobs, like the zombies and the skeletons!

As Steve killed another and picked up the membrane it left behind, he turned towards the village. He needed to ring the bell, to warn the villagers to head inside! Where was Roger when he needed him? All the nitwit did was ring the bell, and now that Steve needed it rung, the green-jacketed villager was nowhere to be found.

"I'm supposed to be retired!" Steve exclaimed, smacking his fist against the bell. The handful of villagers who had been out walking around all bolted into their houses and slammed their doors, looking nervously out the windows at Steve as yet another winged monster dropped down from the sky to bite at him. "OUCH!"

As Steve jumped onto a block to get a better shot at one of them, he noticed something. Not in the village, not in the fortress, but off in the trees of the nearby forest. Light!

"First pillagers, then the sheep, then weird flapping things!" Steve shouted to no one, not at all caring if the villagers thought he was being silly.

"Now this!"

There was only one thing a light out in the woods could mean - fire. Steve hadn't heard a thunderstorm, but he had been pretty deep underground for a while, so there was a chance it had stormed while he was mining. A lightning strike could burn down a whole forest, and then what? He would have to go collect saplings from some distant forest and replant the whole thing! It would be a nightmare, and not at all relaxing like retirement was supposed to be.

"Reeeeh!" A mob screeched, sounding like a burst of steam next to Steve's ear.

"Ouch!" Steve said again, jumping away from the monster and slashing out with his diamond sword. The thing screamed and fell to the ground. How many more were there? Why were they only attacking him?? What could he possibly have done to deserve all this?

Grabbing a bucket from one of the nearby chests, Steve filled it with water from the well, and started off at a run towards the woods. He was exhausted from fighting, and as he opened the gate to leave the village he paused to rifle through his belongings and find a piece of cooked fish. If the cat wasn't going to eat it, he might as well, Steve supposed, even though he didn't very much like the taste of fish. He would rather have traded it with a villager for emeralds, but it did the job and sated his gurgling stomach.

"REEEEEEHHHHHH!"

"Would you go away?!" Steve said, waving his sword around. "You're more annoying than Roger!"

Which was saying something. Roger was the most annoying creature in the entire world. Except for this mob, of course, and maybe that really big salmon Steve had spent half of a morning trying to catch in a frozen river several weeks back.

To Steve's relief, the fire didn't seem to be spreading very fast, or if it was, he couldn't actually see it doing much. Oddly, it didn't even really look like a fire from here. Perhaps the pillagers had frightened a creeper, which had blown a hole into a lava pit? Whatever it was, Steve knew he had to take care of it. Lava had the potential to light nearby trees on fire, and the fire could spread to the village.

Although, Steve thought, it would serve Roger right if his house burned down. Of course, then Steve would have to be the one to rebuild it. It wasn't like Roger could build, and he sure wasn't counting on the pillagers to show up and fix it.

No, Steve was alone in that responsibility. He was the only hero and the only true builder in the world now!

Except whoever had built that staircase, but he wasn't worrying about that right now.

The mobs continued to flap their wings and scream overhead, a spooky noise that gave Steve the shivers as he wandered into the woods. Fortunately, not much else seemed to have spawned out in the dark. There was one brief encounter with a zombie wearing a leather helmet, but the diamond sword made quick work of it.

As Steve reached the glow, he came to a stop. The light, he discovered, was not caused by a pool of lava or a forgotten torch or even a small fire caused by a lightning strike. Tucked up under the edge of a birch tree was a furnace. That in itself wasn't unusual. Steve was always making crafting tables and furnaces and chests and leaving them out in the world and forgetting to pick them up later. They were easy to make, and wood wasn't in short supply, so what did it matter? It was also a nice surprise to find a crafting table he had left behind when he was wandering around.

The unusual thing about the furnace was that it was glowing.

Someone had stocked the furnace with coal, Steve discovered looking into it. It was cooking a stack of fish. Twenty pieces had already cooked, and more were cooking.

"Hang on… Are those my fish?" They had to be! In addition to being the world's hero and only builder, Steve had never seen a villager go fishing.

"No," said a voice from behind Steve, sounding rather smug. "You're not the only one who knows how to fish, you know."

"Oh…" said Steve. He turned. He shouted, one of the creatures overhead screeched, and the furnace popped an ember as if to add its voice to all the noise. Somewhere in the distance, there was the "ZOOP" sound of an enderman teleporting away.

Standing under an oak tree and holding Steve's enchanted diamond sword was a person.

A person, Steve realized. A real, live person, like he was a person. Steve's jaw all but hit the floor. She looked like him! Well, not exactly like him! But her face! A thousand thoughts rushed through Steve's mind. It was too many thoughts, way too many.

"I've got a headache," Steve said, blinking.

She laughed, her square mouth just like his. "You act like you've never seen another person before!"

"I haven't," he confessed. "I think I need to sit down. Obviously, everything that has happened today has caused me to see things."

"Oh yeah, sorry I took your stuff. Those pillagers used up a lot of my supplies," she said, throwing Steve's sword to the ground in front of him.

"I hope you're not mad at me. I'm Alex!"

For a minute, Steve wasn't sure what to say. What was an Alex? "I'm Steve," he said finally, picking up his sword. "Thanks." Why was he saying thank you? He should be shouting at her! She had stolen his things! She -

"Oh, I know." Alex took another step closer. She was very similar to him. A little smaller, but her face was flat like his, instead of bulky and pointing out like a villager's. Her hair was longer, and red, but then villagers didn't have any hair at all! Her shirt even kind of looked like Steve's did, even if it was green instead of blue. Steve couldn't help but stare at her.

It had to be stress, Steve thought. He needed retirement more badly than he realized. All the stress of being a hero had clearly fried his brain. He was hallucinating. That had to be it.

Steve blinked. What had she said? "What is it you know?"

"That you're Steve!" Alex grinned. "I came here to find you and take you back to the city with me."

"The what?" Steve felt like he was doing a lot of blinking, but then, he had never really been surprised before. He remained vaguely aware of the mobs screeching above.

"You really should go to sleep so that the phantoms don't keep coming back," Alex replied, gesturing up to the sky and the winged things floating around.

Steve felt annoyed. Who was she to tell him, the hero Steve, what to do? What was a phantom?? "What city?"

Now Alex was the one looking confused. "You mean you don't know?"

"I don't know what!?" Was she trying to make him feel stupid on purpose?

"The city of builders, Steve!"

"But I am the only builder," Steve replied, now definitely feeling stupid.

Alex laughed once more. It was much different than the sounds the villagers made, or the zombies with their grunting. In some way, it was almost familiar. Steve rubbed awkwardly at the back of his head, wishing one of the phantoms would get through the trees and attack so he could have a distraction.

How could he, Steve the hero, not be the only builder?

www.ingramcontent.com/pod-product-compliance
Lightning Source LLC
Chambersburg PA
CBHW020515030426
42337CB00011B/401

9 781946 525697